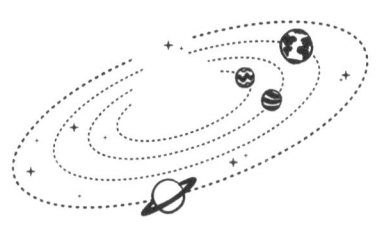

HOW DO YOU WEAR
THE UNIVERSE?

POEMS & ESSAYS
2002-2025

Steve Zeitlin

36 Henry W. Dubois Dr., #8
New Paltz, New York 12561
646-456-3606
MediacsBooks.com

Cover Art by Elaine Norman
Cover and Interior Design by Chloe Annetts

How Do You Wear the Universe?
ISBN 979-8-9991491-3-8

For my children
Ben and Eliza

May they wear their universe
snuggly

ALSO BY STEVE ZEITLIN

JEWels: Teasing Out the Poetry in Jewish Humor and Storytelling
(JPS//U. of Nebraska Press, 2023)

The Poetry of Everyday Life: Storytelling and the Art of Awareness
(Cornell University Press, 2016)

Hidden New York: A Guide to Places that Matter, ed. Steve Zeitlin
and Marci Reaven (Rutgers University Press, 2006-2002)

I Hear America Singing in the Rain: Poems 1968-2002
(First Street Press, 2002)

*Giving a Voice to Sorrow: Personal Responses to Death and
Mourning,* with Ilana Harlow (Penguin-Putnam, 2001)

Because God Loves Stories: An Anthology of Jewish Storytelling
(Simon & Schuster, 1996)

I've Been Working on the Subway: An Oral History of Transit
(NYC Transit Museum, 1992)

City Play, with Amanda Dargan (Rutgers University Press, 1990)

The Grand Generation: Memory, Mastery, Legacy, with Mary
Hufford and Marjorie Hunt (University of Washington Press/
Smithsonian Institution, 1987)

A Celebration of American Family Folklore, with Amy Kotkin and
Holly Cutting-Baker (New York: Pantheon Press, 1982)

BOOKS FOR YOUNG READERS

*The Four Corners of the Sky: Creations Stories and Cosmologies
from Around the World* (New York: Henry Holt, 2000)

*Cow of No Color: Puzzle Stories and Justice Tales from World
Traditions*, with Nina Jaffe (Henry Holt, 1998)

*While Standing on One Foot: Puzzle Stories and Wisdom Tales
from Jewish Tradition*, with Nina Jaffe (Henry Holt, 1993)

Ah life! Everybody has their journey.

— Linda Kleinbub

The Intergalactic Diamond Cloak

How do you wear the universe?

Does it drape across your shoulders
loose
or snug?

Are you lost in it?
Does it need some alterations?

Can you find some warmth in there?

Is it a tattered coat — thrown across your shoulder
or are you —
life-resplendent
in your intergalactic diamond cloak?

CONTENTS

Disproving Death

ESSAYS

INTRODUCTION
The Unified Theory of Everything

In the years 1905 to 1917, while still in his 20s and 30s, Albert Einstein famously published his astonishing theories of special and general relativity that changed the way humanity understood the universe. For his remaining years, he conducted a search for a "unified field theory," combining gravity with electromagnetism and quantum mechanics. It was a search for the "holy grail of physics." The playfully-named "theory of everything" would unify the macro and the micro, explain the movement and actions of the largest things in the universe like stars and planets, and the smallest things in the universe — atomic particles, and, later, quantum. This launched his thirty-year voyage that he hoped would show that these two forces are really manifestations of one grand, underlying principle that could be expressed in a formula as beautiful and simple as the breakthrough equation that came to him in his younger days: $e=mc2$. It's a mystery he never solved.

No Einstein, I too, have failed to solve the mystery.

But I too have my theories.

Here, these theories are poems taking on the valences of life — the everyday, along with unsolvable mysteries of sex and love, and a series of pieces that seek to disprove death. The hypothesis is that I exist — and continue to exist beyond my lifetime — because I had these thoughts set down with structure that secures them in time on a backdrop flimsy as paper. Perhaps it's only a proposition, a set of assumptions about the world for which this book itself serves as proof.

Some years ago, for Fathers' Day, my wife, folklorist Amanda Dargan, presented me with a copy of It *Must Be Beautiful: Great*

Equations of Modern Science. Farmelo compares Einstein's $e = mc2$ to an all-powerful poem. As I read his book, Keats's famous line from "Ode on a Grecian Urn" popped into my head: "Beauty is truth, truth beauty, — that is all / Ye know on earth, and all ye need to know." Keats's *beauty = truth; truth = beauty and Einstein's $e = mc2$* both have explanatory powers in the real world from different vantage points. Einstein's equation explains the relationship of energy, matter, and the speed of light; Keats's elucidates the power, allure, and seeming permanence of art. Keats's formula is written in the English language, Einstein's in the language of mathematics. Although they don't often use the word *truth*, scientists seem to be looking for the same elegant simplicity in their mathematical language as poets seek in words.

Obviously, I am neither Keats nor Einstein (After all, to paraphrase an old Jewish saying, if I were either one — why who would be me?).

Yet like a scientist seeking to explain our universe in simple formulas, I seek to explain my existence in the simplicity of short poems. For decades, ever since college, I have begun my days sitting in an armchair with an old Olympia typewriter or Mac laptop on my knees, writing poetry. I consider it a form of centering, looking into a different kind of mirror, not to comb my hair, but to remind myself of who I am. To create the best version of myself, perhaps. I may have set a world record for time spent — my happiest hours.

My chief inspirations were not only the simplicity of scientific formulas, but the short English lyrics scrawled in the margins of Medieval epics and religious tracts which I discovered in the *Norton Anthologies of British Literature* in high school. Among the classics (which runs through my head after every frustrating day):

O Western Wind when wilt thou blow
The small rain down can rain
Christ! that my love were in my arms
and I in my bed again.

Life is always a poem.

Just a few days ago, Elsa passed away. She was the wife of my good friend, total iconoclast, and photographer, Clayton Patterson. She had suffered from dementia for a decade and he took beautiful care of her. I went to visit, bring some food, and console Clayton, who greeted me with a smile half hidden within a long, wild, braided white beard. While I was sitting in a chair at his Lower East Side home, archive and personal museum, he got a phone call from a friend who asked how he was doing, and he started talking about tides going in and out, along with births and deaths — and how he planned to have the viewing of the body on his birthday, which made some special kind of sense to him. When he hung up, he looked at me and said — "the whole time I was on the phone I could see that you were formulating a poem in your head." How could he possibly have known that? Just as I was leaving, he said, "Well if you write the poem, you should call it 'In Memory of Elsa.'" And I did. (See page 81.)

Clayton envisioning me composing a poem reminded me of how, way back in 2002, soon after I published my first book of poems, *I Hear America Singing in the Rain*, a friend approached me. She said, "I was on the subway this morning, and was amazed to see in the crowded car that someone was actually reading your book of poetry. I thought it was amazing to see someone lost in your poems on the subway. Then suddenly I realized it was you!" Me? Why who better to be reading it?

That year, soon after I published my first book of poetry, I teamed up with Jim Pignetti, a student of mine at Cooper Union, and cofounded the Brevitas poetry group and "school of poetry" dedicated to short poems (fewer than 14 lines). We exchange poems twice a month online, publish an annual anthology and run an annual festival (we're now in our 23rd year). As one early, beloved member, the late Richard Storm, editor of our annual anthology, put it:

On the first and fifteenth of each month, Brevitas poets fill my in-box with whimsy, heartbreak, and delight, all acutely observed in fourteen lines or less. Because the price for receiving these nuggets is to contribute my own, I troll for poetry as I wander through my days.

Richard even wrote about rewards of searching about for poems:

> *Between poems I cast about for the next.*
> *I sift the world, it's all grist:*
> *the dead eyes of a stranger yelling into her phone—*
> *that naked young man in the third-floor window*
> *swigging wine from a bottle....*
> *Even when my net returns empty, the search*
> *connects me— my numbed urban soul revives.*

My favorite poem of his adds more,

> *At a stop light, my morning cab driver looks back*
> *and tells me, "I like your beard."*
> *Mine is white and long, his is short and black.*
> *"I hate to shave and it keeps my face warm," I reply.*
> *"Beard is good," he says, "hides a man's sadness."*

> *You never know when poetry will find you.*

Another Brevitarian, Tanya Beltran, puts it differently, in her lyric, "Where's the Poem."

> *i used to look outside,*
> *into the white wintry mix*
> *of snow and sleet,*
> *and there a poem would be.*
> *i used to speak to a friend*
> *about lovers and exes,*
> *both hes and shes,*
> *and there a poem would be.*
> *i used to sleep and dream*
> *of different worlds and mes,*
> *versions i couldn't believe,*
> *and there a poem would be.*
> *a poem would be.*
> *a poem would be.*

I am deeply grateful to all the Brevitarians who have commented on and helped elevate my poems, particularly Flash Rosenberg, Esther Cohen, Angelo Verga, Cindy Hochman, Jim Pignetti, Gil Fagiani, Christian Garaud, Carolyn Wells, Helen Peterson, Jan Castro, Jan Emerson, Arthur Russell, Amy Barone, Maria Lisella, Ron Kolm, Juanita Torres, Lila Zeiger, Susanna Lee, Tanya Beltram, Tom Rigney, Linda Kleinbub, Karen Neuberg, George Northrup, Mindy Matijasevic, Melinda Levokove, Marjorie Hanft-Martone, Tsaurah Litzky, Jeff Wright, Kathryn Fazio, Leslie Prosterman, and Richard Storm. Bob Holman and my daughter Eliza have added their marvelous touch. I've included two of Eliza's poems, one of them written when she was in kindergarten. Esther Cohen, the world's one and true "book doctor," edited the book. Thanks to Marc Wallace for proof reading. My beloved wife and best friend Amanda made suggestions for many of these poems when they were just a glimmer, and then again when they were almost — as they are always almost

— finished. Martha Dahlen, my dearest friend and editor from California, contributed her abundant creativity to transform and uplift many of these with her passionate love of words. She has been a significant collaborator in the creation of these poems. The wonderful photographer, collage artist, and lifelong friend Elaine Norman designed the dynamite cover, embellished with her Easter Bonnets. Gratitude to Chloe Annetts for the beautiful interior design. Brevies Zev Shanken and Flash Rosenberg, along with Martha, deserve special credit for sending me entire new versions of my own poems, some of which I incorporated into my finished pieces. Poetically, Zev wrote to me,

> *take any phrases you like*
> *to call your own.*
> *send me what you finally use.*
>
> *sports and poetry*
> *are all about*
> *the finished product,*
> *and teamwork*

Hearts and souls — and creativity — of all these loved ones are infused within these pages.

My first book of poetry, *I Hear American Singing in the Rain*, offers up my poetry from 1968, when I was 20, and first began writing short poems, through 2002. *How Do You Wear the Universe*, covers the years since. I asked my friend and wonderful collage artists Elaine Norman to design both covers in parallel with one another. I'm now turning 78. Perhaps it would have been better to publish it on my landmark 75th birthday, or my 80th birthday. Instead, it's on my 75th birthday plus three, and my 80th birthday minus two.

Should you ever be struck by this strange, unusual urge, you can compare the poems I wrote from when I was 20 untill I was 55 in *I Hear America Singing in the Rain* to those I've written from ages 55 till 78 in this volume. I fear that it's hard to keep up with my younger self. A poem from my first poetry book became the title poem of the second, and two other favorites, "Animated Stardust" and the poem now called "Shipwreck" appear in both collections. They are the threaded needles which stitch together the two volumes, the years, and deep-seated experiences of this particular lifespan.

To publish my full collected works of poetry would require waiting till the day I died, and perhaps leaving the task of publishing the book to my kids. Not sure that was a good idea, and not wanting to burden them, I went ahead with this while I still had the energy and time. I thought of leaving a pouch on the final page to slip in any late arriving inspirations.

My own "Unified Theory of Everything" is a series of poems — beginning with a section on writing itself — that seeks to explain and link together — posit my way of understanding — of the physical and spiritual elements of my own being. They make wearing the universe a bit more comfortable. They explain my world to me, and you're invited too.

The Hypothesis of the Short Poem

thanks for inspiration from
George Ella Lyon & Wallace Stevens

I Write

because I never say just what I mean. . .
because that's where my mind wants to go. . .
because I seek a handle on my life. . .

I write
to fill the empty pages of my soul. . .
grasp the fleeting. . .
prove the sentience of being. . .

So I ask the Lord — *give me the nod,*
guide my fingers on the keyboard

for writing —
is the healing hand of God

The Great Whatever

I worked on it forever
seeking to craft The Great Whatever

think outside the box
work my way around the paradox

but I wasn't that clever

in the end, I could not make the world better

up against my limitations —
and the limits of human endeavor

A group poem by Steve Zeitlin & Brevitarians
Bob Holman, Hal Sirowitz, Flash Rosenberg, Jan
Emerson, Susanna Lee, inspiration from Donald
Hall — in honor of the Brevitas poetry collective.

brevitas — the short of it

because there's no string so short it's not worth saving
because this poem is already too long
because attention spans are shortening bread
because a raindrop is as wet as an ocean
because a sonnet is too long and a haiku too short
because short poems have a shape
because long poems crowd the page
because cutting lines is a shave and a haircut
because we get the short end of the stick
because it's not the long but the short of it
because a raindrop is tiny as a tear
because you want to leave them wanting more
because the end is always near

Poets Land

It's raining words in Poets Land
giraffes and hogs in Poets Land
devils and Gods
similes and metaphors
lovers and whores
gigolos and piccolos
crises and a love of
words, evaporating from the pages
raining quiet blows
against the silence
of still water places,
rainwater words, a rain-lit oasis
on desert sands delimits — Poets Land

Once Upon a Time,

My father, plum out of fairy tales,
fashioned a tale about a boy
who woofed down his Cheerios and waited
  for the school bus
then came home to Kraft macaroni and cheese.

I learned to love that storied chum
but it took many nights to comprehend —
that child was me

the tale became — my favorite bedtime story
the woof and warp of days
braided each night before my Dad and I would part

wound by a childhood charmer
who spun life into art.

The Reign of Failure

When your only talent is your thunderous clap
for stars on the stage,
When you can't emit a single woo hoo
    as the curtain falls upon your frozen jaw

When "your only talent is the wanting of talent"
and not a drop was heaven sent,
you walk yourself home for refuge,
contemplate your flaws

Suddenly — a thunderclap!

You slosh on through the deluge
the rain is your applause.

Striptease

Strip the poem down to bare essentials,
tease it into being

Discard falsies and bustier
Let fake fur fall to floor
Strip off all that's crude

Let the words bump and grind
Not even pasties and a g-string
when you're through

The poem stripped, stands nude
You too stand naked
Brood

With a title inspired by folklorist Benjamin Botkin, and family expressions from Beth Hunter, Pete Luckey, Claudia Fugar, and R.A. Stewart Macalister

Folksay

I am from
Yo Sire
and jumping out the fifteenth story window for
  a breeze on a hot day.
From *Tell Ma the boat floats*
to *Too tired to tuck*
from a long story tucked into a family expression
where to sing the hundredth psalm
means to fetch a glass of water,
from the movies we internalized —
the timing that puts us in sync.
I am from the conversations that move from
  prose towards poetry —
rhythm, hyperbole — alliteration —
Thank God for the guts and the gristle
Putting on down to Gourda
Gone, Garfield, gone. . .

the book of steve

she said, *your life means nothing once you're dead*

he said, *no, it's written down*
inscribed onto the cosmos
scrawled in the margins of time

Yes, she said, *but inaccessible to humankind*

yet permanent, still there
like a book. . .

a book nobody reads,
she said

checkpoint

an opening in the barbed wire —
sinister checkpoint
defines a ravaged dreamscape

heart in hand
I present my *Carta de Identidad*
to the uniformed policeman

sheaf of crumpled papers
chronicle of consciousness
proof of existence

I am not here to judge,
he scoffs

then bear witness

he sighs

scribbler, pass by

Family Fusion

Studebaker

Sometimes I feel
I never left the front seat
of my parents' yellow Studebaker —
my eight-year-old self squeezed between Shirley and Irv.

A long drive brought a crazy thought —
how could God possibly exist
if wars killed babies,
heaven is denied to nonbelievers?

Rattled, I urge Dad: *floor the pedal!*
Drive max speed — 60 miles per hour

and that Studebaker hurled roughshod
through my life, past
the Kennedy Assassination, Vietnam, Iraq, Afghanistan,
  Ukraine, Gaza
even the death of my parents,

leaving behind the memory of my young self,
safely squeezed between Mom and Dad
in the absence of God

Maria

I was a 7-year old boy in São Paulo, 1954,
wheezing and gasping for breath in my bed
in the throes of an asthma episode

Shirley and Irv kissed me goodnight
before gallivanting to their evening masquerade —
Dad a French Montmartre painter, Mom a
  Can Can girl.

Our devout Catholic servant Maria
watching me for the night,
hoping that I wouldn't die,
took the cross from round her neck,
placed it on my heaving chest — and prayed.

My Jewish mother bursts through the door —
finds her son peaceful, asleep — yet cringes
at the tiny Catholic cross across my chest —
placed there by a woman who wandered
into our world an angel
masquerading as a maid.

Love & Loss at the Beach

I treasured the sketch books gifted to my 13-year-old self
by the sultry and beautiful Nicole.
Each page, hand drawn, depicted a girl in a bikini,
provided a rush.

She began to lose interest —

desperate and despondent, lovesick
I rode my bike along the beachfront
on the wrong side of the road
looking for Nicole in her bikini strolling on the shore —

Suddenly a car was in my face head on
two headlights and bumper.
I lept wildly from the bike, and watched
the cycle crushed beneath the tires

alive, but sore, I wondered
if love — is to die for

Our Mother's Kiss

As the ball drops before a million at midnight in
  Times Square
a wisp of memory wafts back 10 – 20 no —
  70 years.
My brothers and I were put to bed by 8.
At midnight, our mother would wake us
for a kiss and magic
blessings, wishes for the new year.

Once, too, she woke me up
to ask about my third-grade crush,
and gossiped all through my high school days
asking, who do you love, my dear?
tell me: *who loves who?*

Now, as the ball drops, it's my turn
to wake her from the long dead with a kiss —
join your three boys
— Bill, Murray, Steve —
as the crowd explodes with crazy kisses,
because everybody loves everybody on
  New Year's Eve.

Memory Matters

"On the mercy of memories and the lust for meaning"
~Svetlana Alexievich, *Secondhand Time*

Cynical and unsentimental, my Dad, claimed
to live only in the present,
impatiently moving on,
staring into the future till
he blinked and his Rolleiflex camera clicked.

When I sat with my father at his bedside,
just before he died, he said
Steve, It's all so forgettable.

Today, my brothers and I sit beside the
  boxes, flipping through photos —
square, black and white slivers of memory —
No Dad, it's not "forgettable" —
we have the pix you snapped —
the validation of memory
the construction of memory.
No need to knock — our evanescent eternity

Dali and Dad

The artist, Salvador Dali, called his melted clocks
the Camembert of time

Camembert, my father's favorite cheese
just as Rolex was his favorite watch
Cutty Sark his favorite scotch
Dad was a fan of all things fine —
except, perhaps, his children.

As his hard edges melted down
we recall how his knowledge
took the conversation up a notch,
how his sense of humor rocked

Our time together aged and ripened
like Camembert
like Dali's melted clocks.

One Legged Swimmer at the Beach

Two crutches crossed by the edge of the sea.
Beyond, the one-legged swimmer turns,
swims for deeper waters

I yell, Doug, Doug, you're in too deep!
which is precisely what my father thought
when his good friend asked those fathomless questions:

Is it all about making money, Irv?
What is fidelity anyway?

Though as a child, I sat silent through all
   those conversations,
asking only —
how did you lose your leg?
(and hearing different stories),
I imagined hoisting myself up on your crutches
to see a little further, venture —   into deeper waters

Ode to Silliness

Hit-you-last. You lose.
My brother Murray and I still
greet each other Yo Sire.
Why? Murray answers, Respect

When I do too *much* of anything Murray will say
Why don't you just jump out of the
   15th story window
for a breeze on a hot day?!

And ever since we watched the great white shark
   terrify the folks in *Jaws* one night in 1975
apropos of nothing, Bill will say
Speaking of the Big White. . .

For the life of us, we cannot dance or sing
but we refine our communication into art
heartful sharing becomes artful sharing
The deepest meanings hide in the silliest things.

Getting Dressed

Grandpop Harry taught me
how to tie my tie with a Windsor knot
Uncle Jay to fold a sports coat

My Dad taught me
that a shirt has four separate corners to tuck
My mother Shirley said to hold my sleeves
when putting on a sweater for the cold

Underneath our clothes
Uncle Adolph used to say
We are all naked. . . .

I wear them all each day
Naked, fully clothed

Harry's Seder

Come on and join up
the last of the family reserve.
        ~Lyle Lovett

When I was a boy, Grandpop Harry
  was the family Seder.
When he died of a stroke in 1965, the first
  of nine siblings to die,
Bubby Rose — rose at the Seder and announced,
  tearfully,
poetically — uncharacteristically —
The captain is dead, but the ship must sail on.

Later, cousin Richie took the helm from Harry, asked
Why should this night be different from all other nights?
Aunt Elaine stepped on deck, took the floor —
I think all of us should remember why we're here,
  she said
It's not the suffering of the Jews in Egypt,
It's not to taste the bitter herb
But to remember Grandpop Harry, Daddy Al,
  and Bubby Rose.
They anchored us.

Seders came and went. Bubby Rose passed on.
Aunt Elaine passed away too —
rememberers out to sea with the remembered.

Years later, clambering among the empty deck chairs,
the words of Richie Wallace — no longer with us —
echo across the Seder Hall —
The captain is dead, he says, *the whole crew is gone…*
but the ship must sail on.

Our Brazil

In my high school annual
Jocelyn wrote
Always remember "our Brazil"

Not the Brazil of *cafezinhos,*
barzinhos, bossa nova
or tipping *muleques* on the street
to find a *jeitinyo* so they don't
slash the tires of your car

Just some crazy expats at an international school
in the hinterlands of Morumbi
a beach in Guaruja

50 years, 5,000 miles
yet "Our Brazil" still stays in view

Saudades, Jocelyn
a word emblazoned on your ankle —
your very first tattoo —
a word they say has no translation —
maybe longings, longings,
longings for "our Brazil"

Saudades, friends, forever and until. . ..

Theory of Days

Thoughts on a Windy Beach

If you hold sand too tightly in your hand,
it will run through your fingers.
~ Joni Mitchell, sent as a Dear John telegram to
Graham Nash, 1970

Child of Water and Land
footprints strewn across the sand
I seek to fathom my own life
hold it in my hands

My life cradled like a babe in arms
I frantically seek to understand
how this child winds up an old man,
friends who died by their own hand,
life's uneven span

Bending low, I grasp
a fistful of sand
that slowly
slips
slides
slippery
as moments
drifting
sifting
through
fingers
back into the waters
and the lands

How a Sign at the Edisto Market Becomes a Prayer for my Son, my Daughter, and all the Young Creatures of this Earth

July through September
loggerhead hatchlings
guided by the reflection of the moonlight in the water
make their journey to the sea

Please turn off all lights — porchlights, flashlights,
    car lights — to keep confused hatchlings
from losing their way

for Amanda

Oceans and Eons

Before the tide subsides
leaving its seawash ashore,
Amanda searches for wing shells.
I scour the shore for clamshells
stained in ocean blue

The universe observes two souls in
  search of seashells
leaving patterned footprints in concentric circles,
moving together, then apart

Amidst the chaos of the cosmos,
oceans and eons,
I touch your shoulder.
Look, a shell
in the shape of a heart.

The Human Highlight of the Day

We all know days that end before they start,
days without anything
to set them apart.

Days without a burst of laughter
or the quickening of a human heart.

To resist, I take a glass of wine to bed,
scour the hours of the day
for a memorable remark
hoping for a single bright idea to swoop in on a lark,

so I can sleep, knowing the day
is numbered and marked
by simple human touch
a shared creative spark

Life Span of a Wine Glass

I take a glass of red to bed each night
to contemplate the dimming of the day

make it last by drinking half
hold it steady so it will not tip,
knowing that if I drink half and half and half
— till just a fraction of a sip is left —
then take a sliver of a sip
and then a droplet
the pour will never stop,
the wine flow past eternity —
towards time everlasting,

till we…

raise a wine glass overflowing
never waste a drop

You

tell me — STOP
taking two cups of wine to bed.
Bad for your sleep and your blood pressure.
It will kill you in the end.

Then, knowing my intransigence
send a bottle of Hawthorne extract
to help protect my heart.

So every night
I squeeze the dropper,
watch the magic elixir
disappear into the wine —
forbidden potion!

This the venom, the remedy too,
the kill and the cure —
poison, antidote

and a daily dose of you

for Ben

Underdog

Could a been a World Champ
but he was sorely robbed

tonight — he's ready for another slog

tonight our hero's goin' whole hog

goin' up against the Fighting Frog —
the legendary Overdog.

Oh no! He's tagged by a left.
down for the count
flat on the mat,
head in a fog

proud to retain his Undisputed Heavyweight Title —
Underdog

Close but No Cigar

I still can't remember all the best things she said.
                    ~ Bob Dylan

As your shot just missed the line
in Pickleball, I called out
Close but no cigar — as they say

You answered,
Fuck you — as they say

We crumbled into laughter.

An entire friendship
held together
with a tidbit of humor tumbling from our lips.

Sealed with a quip.

Backstage

Backstage, Juan beats a bomba
on the buleador
before the curtains rise

Shovana, Carnatic singer of ancient songs says
We have the same rhythm —
an ancient connection that we can't neglect.

In Puerto Rican Spanish,
he says, *buleador comes from the word boula —*
it means — to remember

We too speak of the boula
What do you suppose it means in Hindi? she says.
To forget

Birth of Memory

Banished from The Garden, Adam cursed
God, Eden, his own rib, and the apple
Eve had eaten.
He held
her hand too tight as he walked
into the darkness of whatever was to be.

Then Eve turned
for a last glance at the Garden.

Her glimpse unhardened
   Heaven's heart.

God worried —
   death and time are too unkind so
graced them both
with memory.

When the Gods Line Up for Communion

I believe in all the Gods.
~ Jack Santino

With their creations collapsing,
Gods show up for confession.

Long list of sins to right.
Long line to receive communion
from us humble human tykes.

Wine that we proffer
is the soul of humankind
not the blood of Christ.

The Wafer we offer is just a soda cracker
that, dissolving on the tongues of Gods,
forgives their sins, bestows eternal life

Patterns

Tangled yarn in search of patterns
   probing for the needle's eye

Guiding hand of the Goddess Frig on the treadle

Weft and warp of the World Loom —
pegged to corners of the sky
tacked somewhere between Venus and Saturn,

her shuttle threading love and time
stories winding, through and over

a weave of loves and losses
softer when patterned

thanks to Annie Lanzillotto and Zev Shanken

Blood of Time

pierced by a missile, M16 pellet,
arrow, slingshot, or spear,

this time on Ukrainian soil
a dying soldier,
twisted hands across his torso,
seeks to thwart the going of his life,
struggles
to hold his insides in,
as blood of thirty, forty, fifty unlived years
oozes from between his desperate fingers —

drowning his high school ring of love,
his wedding and his children —

universal soldier's sacrifice —
the sacred blood of time.

thanks to Bob Holman

Things that Can't Be Changed

There's no escaping the prison
of things that can't be changed

the murderer cries — rise up dead man!
How'm I live that down?

Low moan condemnation
lockdown of the past.

We shake the bars till we're deranged,
plan our escape — till we're

SHOT

scaling the wall
of all that can't be changed

A Father's Plea

Why must you be, my blue-eyed girl,
prisoner of your own insanity?

Aren't we all? She said to me,
Myself only more so, you see

Yes! I said, as we walk round and round the prison grounds
trapped in our own mentality

But it's not a deep dark mystery

When stark locked gates surround you
check your inside pocket
for the key

Eliza Zeitlin's Blues

A poem written by Eliza Zeitlin in Kindergarten.
"The teacher asked us to write a 'blues,' Eliza said,
"so there were 29 homework blues and this."

I hate it when animals die
I really can't stand it
I just want to cry

I love them so much
I really do
I love the penguin and the kangaroo
I love the frog, the deer, the dolphin

I love them big
I love them small
I don't even know the names of them all

I love the foxes with their beady eyes
I love the birds that fly in the skies
I love the rat
And besides that
I really can't name them all

So let's just put it this way
I love animals!!!

Sympathy for the Empath

Empaths deserve — a little empathy.

When I see an animal in distress, my daughter says,
  I don't just feel sorry for that dog or pig,
I live inside their anguish. Their suffering
  surrounds us

on our plates. On our bathroom shelves.
On the semi-truck. On the highway. Starving
on our streets. In dark forgotten corners. . .
they meet our culture's wrath.

So our beloved girl must live out
her passion and her care,
trying to save Cat. Turtle. Dog. Pig —
each dying animal stumbling across her path,
with scant thought to the aftermath.

She caught the "I Love Animals" blues
and cannot just walk past

Girl Outside

Out front of Macy's, 10 below —
a cloud forms on her breath.
I watch her pretty face, sharp clothes
destined for the good life
next to the doorway, pressed

What anguish, its moment come around,
what lost love, what inner demons
lead her to spark a cigarette
protect the flicker with her palm
suck in her breath
as if the only way to find her calm
is to inhale a measure of her death

for Amanda

Clotheslines of Heaven

When asked to close her eyes
and see the places in her heart where she felt utterly at peace,
Amanda recalls Aunt Eliza's house on the top of
  See Off Mountain,
the first house her great aunt built, named Yanside
 (Yonderside in mountain speak)
in Brevard, North Carolina — beautiful rustic home
where a tree grew through the porch
where Amanda sat at sunrise
looking down into the valley with the clouds below
listening to a goat, climbing up the mountainside
its bells tinkling.

Or a moment on the farm before sunset
hiding in the winter rye, playing hiding-go-seek,
looking up at the sky and the clouds
hearing her cousins laughing
knowing she would soon be caught
but wasn't caught yet

Perfect moments strung like white sheets
drenched with pure, rainwater memories
along the clothelines of heaven

The Highwire of Heaven

Don't confront me with my failures,
I have not forgotten them.
                    ~ Jackson Browne

balancing on the highwire
strung out across the sky. . . .

in my right hand — the weight
of all that's been accomplished

in my left, the heft of all I've left undone
before my days are through

the kindnesses I might have shown,
women I should have once made love to

As I swerve to hold the two in balance
I — stumble —
like all of us — left
hanging — dangling —
from the highwire of heaven

The Fucking Past

clamoring to be remembered,
tailing me

with a torrent of papers and photos,
tsunami of memories
tempest of memorabilia

tornado
swirling in the attic

river of forgetter's guilt
threatening to drown me
in decisions right and wrong

all I could have purchased for a song

in the crest of the crash of the past
I cry

Get back, get back
— as the Beatles sang —
get back to where you once belonged

If You're So Lucky as to Live

a good life, a full and sweet life
then live and love it fully
thankful you were
never raped or abused
never lived on the streets
never stabbed for your race or religion
never ran for the bomb shelter
never had to kill those you oppose —
never had a child who took his own life.

You need to live for all of those luckless souls —
may their souls find solace in yours

Tilt Your Mirror

On this eyelash of an island
on this planet of precarity
Tilt your mirror

to see the dead alive again
spot the bomb inside a can
restore the blind to sight
blind your enemies with light
Tilt your mirror

if you don't like your looks or style
Tilt your mirror

to see your lover's eyes alight
redirect a beam of light
set the flooded world afire
light the tragic funeral pyre
Tilt your mirror

to see beyond what's happened here
or make it all disappear
Tilt your mirror

A Universe of Stories

based on the work of folklorists
Kay Turner and Americo Paredes

Why Witches Fly

Every story needs a witch
and in this Mexican tale
the Witch Wife sheds her skin
and flies away each night

The jealous husband tracks her footsteps
to find out where she flies
then stumbles upon the place she hides
her crinkled skin

He salts and burns
leaves a smoldering heap
of blistering skin on the floor,
then blithely waits for her return

But she never returns to him.
He learns
why witches fly

Because they're free

traditional tale found in many of the world's cultures.
In India it's often called "The Mustard Seed."

Cup of Soil

In India, a young woman gives birth to a baby girl
who dies, soon after, in her arms.
She carries the tiny corpse from town to town
asking for medicine to revive her baby girl.

A holy man promises a cure:
He says: *All I will need is a cupful of soil. . . .*

A cupfull of soil? No problem at all.

from a house, the healer says,
where none has experienced the sorrow of death

Babe in arms, she travels door to door
to the houses of the rich, the poor
in search of that simple cup of soil.

She hears, I lost a son. I lost my parents.
 I lost my husband.
The dead are many, the living few.

At last, she summons resolution,

travels to the boneyard outside town
buries her baby girl — cup of soil by cup of soil —
in the cold, cold ground.

thanks to the Taproot Program of the
Alliance for California Traditional Arts

The Tradition Bearers

We "mus tek cyear a de root fa heal de tree" —
We must take care of the roots to heal the tree.
~ Gullah Geechee Proverb

Tradition bearers
are the trees of any culture.
roots going back generations,
gnarled, tested by
generational instability,
incessant gusts of social change
the slow erosion of time.

Like all of us,
their traditions are as fragile as flowers in the storm
holding out as long as they can
seeds and petals whooshed into the tempest, tossed,
giving up their beauty
hoping someone somewhere someday
reaches for a fading petal blowing past
  upon a softening breeze
picks up where they left off

Thanks to Rabbi Edward Schecter

Why Good People Do Bad Things

Listen child, did you just drag a crayon
across the wall of this lovely pizzeria?

Do you think
that was a good idea?

No, she said,

Do you think
it was a smart idea?

No, it was a terrible idea.

Then why'd you do it?

cause when I did it
I thought it was a good idea

How to Ruin a Dead Cat Joke

A partly true story

Alissa came home from school
and could not find Cheesie, her kittycat.

She saw a sign on the refrigerator door,
Don't open the freezer, Cheesie's inside.

Mom, Cheesie's in the freezer?

Alissa, we need to talk.
Sadly the cat died —
that's why we had to put her in the freezer.
Now she's in heaven with Grandma.
I'll leave it at that.

You mean she's not in the freezer?

She's with God in heaven, Alissa.

Mom! Why are you telling me that?

What on earth
would God want
with a dead cat?

Coming Soon, the Great Gu-Zamba

The pitchman's credo: first you must have something to sell.
Second, you have to make it seem 10 times greater than it
really is.
> ~ Carnival and medicine show pitchman, T.P. Kelly

In one of the great ruses,
the legendary pitchman, T. P. Kelley, in his travels
comes upon the next small town — Zebulon,

papers the walls with posters —

THE GREAT GU-ZAMBA IS COMING!!

Crazed with curiosity, the town's fascination grows,
wondering if the beast hailed from the Amazon.

On the day of the promised performance
he modifies the signs to say —

THE GREAT GU-ZAMBA IS HERE!

That night the theater is packed with paying customers
hell-bent to see the touted oddity.
At 9:29, a steam whistle shrieks

as a southbound train makes its local station call.
A shadowy figure hops aboard.
The crowd sits, transfixed, awaiting SHOWTIME!

At precisely 9:30, the curtains rise!
The huckster journeys on.
A poster center stage reads

THE GREAT GU-ZAMBA HAS GONE!

Bad News

Did you read about it in the paper?
Mother asked Dad
Oh that poor child — hit by a car.

At the age of 5, I overheard.

If I am careful crossing the street, I ask
and don't take candy from strangers
I'll never die, will I?

You know we all die, Mom said.

WHAT! I screamed,
befuddled and confused.

So I waited by the elevator
for my two sisters to arrive

Girls, I said
I have some very bad news. . . .

Tenets of Science

The Big Bang
Revisited, Revised

The Big Bang
precedes
the yin yang,
I tell my Taoist friend.

Why, she says,
do men
contend
explosives
are the center of everything?

Women give birth,
Men come in bursts, I declare.

For me it's more a whisper than a shout,
she answers.
In Tao the beginnings are always everywhere —

across the fertile plains of endlessness
The Big Sprout

Celestial Intensity

Aimar said, "I love everyone—
just at varying distances."

Like galaxies in a universe —
we are each — a solar system —
people we know — asteroids, shooting stars,
maybe comets, coming, then going
below, around, above.

Those who venture too close. burn up,
while others, too far, drift away

When the space between is perfectly calibrated,
you're a planet,
fixed in orbit, held in place
by the gravitational force we call love.

Sacred Triangle

Ancient astronomical calculations: the distance
between the bright stars of the summer triangle —
 Vega, Altair, Deneb —
some say, inspired the sacred triangle of ancient
 Greek Temples —
Aphaia on the island of Aegina
Poseidon at Cape Sounion
Parthenon on the Acropolis in Athens
dedicated to Athena, Goddess of Wisdom,
 born from the head of

Zeus, who fell in love with the lovely Callisto,
disguised himself as her friend, the Goddess Artemis
raped the mortal beauty.

Vengeful Hera, wife of Zeus, transformed the lovely
 young woman to a bear,
outlined in the sky around the brightest stars of
 the summer triangle
in a place no God could reach her, demonstrating
symmetry between heaven and earth, gods and mortals,
souls lost to the stars — surrounding us each night.

The Line

In these moments of exquisite existence
I tread the line
where past and future intersect —
my preciously guarded present —
hairbreadth of a line
pressed between what's ahead and what's behind.

I inhale the future, exhale the past
to keep the sides apart

till late one year, the line disappears —
in my absence — past and future reconnect
regardless of my tears.

for Henry Chalfant, inspiration
from Caroline Harris

Crooked Time

The only reason for time, Einstein said,
is so everything doesn't happen at once.

but the sculptor disagrees.

Resurrecting a piece of his childhood
he lodges it catty corner to his midlife crises.
Zig zagging the years
with a jigsaw,
he wedges old age in
before his adolescence,
spray-paints it all
with lovers, from high school to assisted living
in reverse

dubs his masterpiece

time all at once

In Memory of Elsa
or
Rhythm of Time

When Elsa, his wife of too many years to count
(except for the ones defined by dementia)
passed away
Clayton spoke to me
with sentiments too sad to say.

He began with the obvious
talked about ebb and flow
waxing and waning
births and burials

To give tides and lives duration,
we agreed,
the universe created time

bequeathed to time — a rhythm —
tones and stresses from spans that intertwine
spoken in heartbeats and drums
tears and tarantellas

So Clayton buried Elsa on his birthday
making sense out of the cadence
her death a syncopated note in time

Quantum Entanglement

two particles — twins
separated at birth — still shape one another's
 position, momentum, spin

action at a distance.
Einstein called it senseless
unscientific, newfangled

but mystics knew it had to be,
poets understood intuitively

how you could be so far way
our lives still so entangled

Paradox of Proof

And God, as promised, proves / to be mercy clothed in light
                    ~ Jane Kenyon

God declares, *Let there be light*
Eons later, Einstein responds —
Let there be particles and waves

Michael Guillen, scientist and man of faith,
claims — *if light can be particle and wave*
Jesus can be both mortal and immortal.

God, he wrote, is light, *that became particle*
in the flesh and blood of Jesus — truth larger than
proof.

I can't make that leap of faith through Guillen's
portal.

yet at times I feel both mortal and immortal.

Black Hole

Stephen Hawking illuminated Black Holes,
swirls of such immense gravity that nothing —
  not even light — can escape.
A person or spaceship flying in whooshes
  into nothing.

Sally knew nothing of Black Holes till she
discovered that her lover,
aging with Parkinson's
could no long remember their affair
recalled nothing, not even quips,
    the soulful kisses, laughter....

Suddenly, she understood the nature of Black Holes.
Heartbreaking gaps in her universe,
black hole of forgetfulness
that could one day swallow the whole.

When Sol Gave Up Hope
of Finding Answers

he discovered
that when he asked a question,
his mind was both accessible and engaged.

Because the universe is an open question —

inquiry provides protection
from the ignorance of certainty.

Raising the world's consciousness with answers
is too big a lift!

for the whole universe
is God's ongoing answer
to the question
"What if?"

Animated Stardust

Sentient being,
Are we on a quest to understand the universe
Or are we some aspect of creation's quest
To understand itself?

Frail and human creatures of the cosmos
Can we sense the presence
Of our own creator

In this animated stardust?
This dust that renders visible
A stream of light —

Particles dancing in a beam of light!

Valences of Sex and Love

Our Saving Grace

Love is a ribbon not a rope, Babe

Love is not a buckle
That fastens you to me

Love is a guess,
A breakable promise
A kiss, a hickey
Not a tattoo

Love is my only gift to you

True — it's our best and only hope.
Yet love is a ribbon, not a rope

Old Poem, Reconsidered

my world is flat
but lit by a golden arc.

beneath I chart my place of birth,
the location of my death.

the women I have loved
illuminate my trek,

brighter towards the fall of night
like suns, that rise — but never set.

Amanda, barefoot by the stream

If you have a dear companion
and you know her soul within
you can walk her back to childhood
as if you knew her then —

I watch you by the winding stream
pick the berries and the fruits
placing secrets for the fairies
between the cypress roots

With cousins lined on haystacks —
you teach them their 3 Rs
They all learn from you, Amanda —
teacher that you are

With streams and lessons flowing,
the grass on your bare feet,
we tease each other endlessly
and know one day we'll meet

You roam the woods for hours
and never lose your way,
cross the bridge down by the schoolhouse
to walk to school each day

where you'd let a boy hold all your books
If you were so inclined.
Today I'll haul your weathered books
across the bridge of time

Sour Cream Potato Soup

After my surgery,
Amanda stood in the doorway with a pot
  of sour cream potato soup

then brought me to her bed in Philadelphia.

assumed my faults and fetishes
were foibles
distilled my essence
in her stories

so that some say she did not cry
but reached up and clasped

— my fleeting soul —

the day I died.

Robyn

when your wisp of a body stood on my feet in the dorm
your finger traced lines across my chest

Three words.
Two hearts.
One flutter away
From never again.

Now in the never again
I tease you,
say I can't recall the three lost words.

They could be any three words, you laugh,
and, anyway, to say those words aloud
would scare the birds away

thanks to Shelley Posen

Swan's Wing

A friend once said — mention a swan —
you'll get a predictable response —
a swan can beat a man to death with its wings —

this became our expression
for bringing up the same old thing
we called it the flapping of a "swan's wing."

Things that were simply not worth mentioning
things beneath the "threshold of interest"
were below the "T of I"

There's no need to tell me everything,
or give me reasons why
but when you lean in and whisper

unexpected things

surprise
lifts me higher
than a swan can fly

Deep Water Friend

Adrift in deeper waters
we grapple with life's questions

our world goes topsy turvy —
feet tickling an ocean of sky.

Awash in ideas and hypotheses,
we dive toward a dark world beneath —
through kelp, seagrass, seaweed,
fish in schools of nonsense,
shipwrecks, bones, treasure —
a history of humanity written on the sea bottom.

And when we again break through for air
it's only for a moment — a gasp, a few breaths —
some surface chatter
before returning to the murky, safe depths

Litmus Test of Love

If only there were indicator strips
to test a love, reveal the secrets
of its chemistry

test the possibility
that you loved too little or too much

Put your lips against the strip —
a lick of vinegar — or wine?

does it turn blood red —
is it a short-lived flash fire —
like the love at our drive-in movie's "Passion Pit"

or blue — slow-burning ember
destined to deepen far beyond desire

The true test is when you put your lips to mine.

dark light

wash away your inhibitions
divulge the naked urge

haunt the dark places
where spirits troll

for inebriated laughter
in the lipstick's red glow

no one casts a shadow

the light shines from below

Sacred Trust

"If you work out the sexual cues with one another, well, then
you have your own private language, just the two of you —
you're keeping the secrets of the relationship."
~ Julia Hutton, Good Sex

Our relationship is built on secrets
tucked in whispers and sighs

secrets of what drew us together
in this strange duet —

secrets to what gives me pleasure
what makes you come

Can you promise never to forget?
Can you keep us free of all regrets?

Can you keep the sacred secret
now that it all has come undone?

Perfect Love

Sitting across from you at a restaurant table
when all the ions are charged
and I'm in the zone with you —
in the ozone just above your eyes

your spirit comes wafting into view

As we speak
our spirits promenade
down Second Avenue
dance on restaurant tables
criss-cross rivers and bridges
zip across the skyline
like some crazed angels from above
our spirits galavanting
making perfect love

Shipwreck

Will you share my sweet, sweet memories
of the pain?
(sadistic separation of souls)

Or will you regret
one treasured moment of our pirated pleasure —
ask me to discipline our bad, bad girl

Bind you to the bed posts

Lash you to a ship's mast
Set the rigging aflame!

Save you with a barrage of kisses
like a downpour of rain.

Treatise on Love

There are two kinds of people in the world,
Those I like and those I love.

For me, it's different, you say,
There are those I like, and those I tolerate.

I guess we're leaving out the ones we hate.

Here's what's at stake —

If I love those who don't love me
I suffer endless heartbreak.
If I am loved by those whose love I don't return
for whose love I never yearned
I'm left with nothing but a bad headache.

Give those other folks a shove
for all that truly matters
is to be loved by those we love.

Triumph of Intimacy

the day that passion pays our rent
the day we laugh when our money's spent

the day you find your mother's arms
the day mom's love makes the thug disarm

the day warring couples reconcile
the day we forgive those we revile

the day our enemies break bread
the day our love brings back the dead

the day you're unafraid to kiss me —
the triumph of intimacy

Old Girlfriends

Every ten or twenty years,
surprisingly you reappear
to run your needle through the fabric of my days

clothing us in memories

your woven wisp of voices whisper
across intermittent time

patching the gaps,
patterning our lives,
threading the years

The Gift

When my funds can't solve your problems
Your life is hanging by a thread
When all options are exhausted
When you can't get out of bed
When what's gone down can't be defended
When nothing can be changed
When what's torn cannot be mended
The pieces rearranged

When the bus has left the station
When the train is off the track
When you find there's no way forward
No way of turning back

When you feel your life is worthless
When you've moments left to live
I stand before you helpless. . .
Love is all I have to give
Love is all I have to give

Sequence of Souls

Shot of Time

Come gather round dear friends and lovers
Hail an accident of birth
How by chance we came to share
This moment here on earth

This old world just keeps on turning
Linked in time we take our turn
The time we spend is all we earn
No refunds, no returns

Raise a glass to all these moments
I'll drink to yours, you drink to mine
I might have missed you sweetheart if
The stars had not aligned

Bottom's up, this pub is closing
You handsome men, you pretty girls
Kiss the one who's nearest you
'Fore you leave this crazy world

Raise a glass to all these moments
I'll drink to yours, you drink to mine
Take a swig for all the years
As we down this shot of time

Rod

My cousin Rod McIver — smoke jumper —
parachuted into Missouri wildfires
became famous for escaping the great Montana blaze
by igniting a flickering ring of fire round himself,
hunkering down so the
sea of flames —
passed over and around

teaching us — when the infernos of the body politic
hurl down upon your fragile soul
light a passionate, flickering, fiery circle
round yourself, your family, friends

let the fires of this wicked world
pass over

Lucas #1

cradled loblolly logs in his arms
and taught us the secret of lightwood —
a knot thick with resin
in the heartwood of the dying tree

kindling
for reflection and thought

a mind that grasps the world
the way an axe cleaves wood
memory like the rings of an old trunk
humor popping like greenwood in the fire
heartwood of the family tree

Lucas #2

When he died
we buried him
in a hole
that could never be filled.

Eliza

sprightly imp
squeezed into this world sideways
hung her pictures
at a slant
balanced the box
on its side
at an angle
on a tilt
askew
about to tip
shimmying
along the rim
teetering
on the edge
legs splayed
arms akimbo
feet awry
she named her cat "Slightly"
took herself lightly —
that's the only way angels can fly

The Miracle of Benh and Mel

My brother Benh was a cherubic child.
His fat, overripe cheeks hung from his face like
    August peaches.
They sprang into action at the slightest joy, which he found
everywhere,
    from an empty cardboard box to the cracks in the
    asphalt alley.
Together, we lived a life of high adventure on the sidewalks
    of New York.

Looking over this joyful childhood was the ever-creeping
  shadow of Growing Up,
    like a monster under the bed, visible only to children in
    the room.
Puberty hit like a sledgehammer,
    and I watched with horror as my compatriot withdrew
    into the gathering darkness of adolescence.

One morning he emerged from his room, and to my
    absolute shock

THE CHEEKS WERE GONE

The last vestige of childhood — vanished.

As the years whirred by, I discovered that, though puberty
    is mandatory,
Growing Up is optional.

Years passed.
Benh proposed to the lovely Melanie Akoka atop the
    Coney Island Cyclone Roller Coaster
sealing the deal with a peach pit ring
created by scraping it on the sidewalk —
    a New York street kids' tradition.

When Benh and Mel stepped off the Cyclone beaming
we witnessed the miracle

THE CHEEKS HAD RETURNED

Bill

We teased my brother Bill —
Read a book! we'd say. *Read a book!*
Now grown, we marvel
that he can remember events, dates, times
as though his mind were a box of photographs
each labeled, dated, filed —

like the day we first saw *Jaws* — Christmas, 1975
at the Gemini Theater on Rua Paulista
after lunching with our friends, the Beamans —
events that slip through my mind like a sieve.

We didn't know the path Bill would take
but he has a perfect sense of direction,
able to drive us home,
deep into the past
to places where we still live.

Linda

bolts out of Cuthbert, Georgia, onto the stage at Yale,
plays Puck in *Midsummer Night's Dream* opposite
  Meryl Streep
her gruff tone resonant as Bogart's offering blunt advice

We see her as a judge on *Law and Order* —
more often from an armchair
holding court
with vivid gestures, wry wisdom, sage advice

You'll never meet anyone like her twice!

Teaches convicts how to act, speaks her mind to local cops
never shies away from strife

on her back porch every night, lights
a single cigarette
to preserve one single vice —

Linda's singular portrayal of a life.

Selina

Grew up beside her Abuelita
Jerusalén Morales, espiritista,
who opened a botanica in the Bronx —
pharmacy for the soul

Wherever she went, Selina would follow
helped her wrap copper coins in red cloth
tie them with a slim white ribbon
peddle "lucky pennies" for a dollar

Through the hands of a healer, the spirit flows —
unencumbered, her Abuelita said —
help people address their inner being
or find their lucky number

Teresa

Stayed up nights, held back a yawn —
the jig-saw puzzle still undone —
no graceful image of a swan to greet the dawn

It's the jagged edges of my life
pieces that never fit together
I'm unfinished! I'm —
she swoons, as in the movies —
Good as gone!

Teresa — the search for grace goes on and on
Drift with the darlings
Don't sweat the swan

for the artist Elizabeth Murray

Elizabeth

cut canvases apart
reimagined hearts
as curves and triangles
reassembled parts

her advice:
get married, have kids —
that's the best part —

ah, to know the painter and her painting
the artist — and her art

Amanda

A baby
born
anywhere
always
makes
her
smile

Annie

Created the pick-me-up-box
floating in a cloud of sadness

When the gales of grief blow the wooden lid ajar —
recipe for the world's best chocolate chip cookie
awaits

Sweet words from your daughter on a voicemail
I'm so happy you're my Mom

This box is always there for you, Annie.
Hovering in a cloud of sadness, it never locks.
I pray it picks-you-up
when you place this poem in the box

Aunt Mary Hart

if you ever want to surprise Aunt Mary Hart
tell her the time

with such a busy life
only time could slow her down till

arthritis made her fingers gnarl —
she couldn't even grasp a pencil

bones and heart
in fading cotton

she climbed upstairs, cleaned her attic
of old student papers
to get herself in a "dying condition"

Yet when the Reaper whispered — "time"
did a shiver of surprise
run down her spine?

Nonnie

A bobbing cork
adrift upon the ocean
message in the bottle
lost

That's how I see my gypsy self, she sighed,
tipsy, holding court.

Popped from a bottle of champagne!
I cried
overflowing, tossed upon a bubbling froth

Just then her cocktail spills — a splash
essence of her being
on her blouse —
exuberance uncorked!

Aunt Elaine & Judy Garland

In the restroom of the Rainbow Grill
Aunt Elaine claimed she glimpsed
the famous Judy Garland
as she ducked into a stall

called out above the door
I don't want to seem crass, Miss Garland
but when you sing 'Somewhere Over the Rainbow'
tears well in my eyes
Your singing's unsurpassed.

Lady, she replied,
I've got rainbows coming out of my ass

Christine

When we sat together in the park,
discussing Roland Barth's Camera Lucida, you asked
When I take your picture does it change both you and me
hmmmmmmmm?

I believe — and want to know if you believe —
stone carving, weaving and music
are forms of non-alphabetic writing systems
for cultural memories
hmmmmmmmmm?

And that needlework, too, can be a form of spirituality
hmmmmmmmmm?

Suddenly I knew that to love this woman
I need not know the answers,
nor understand the questions
simply tune into the melody
hmmmmmmmmm

Annie Lanzillotto

took as her metaphor the spaldeen, the New York City ball.
Spaldeens, she wrote, *took on the smell of the street.*
Spaldeens sweated and got dirty.
spaldeens taught her soul to find adventure, to fly, to roll, to
hide, to float, to be buoyant —
    and to bounce back.

Annie! Immunocompromised, quarantined, hospitalized
with double pneumonia, deflated immune system,
  recurring tumors
from Hodgkin's lymphoma at 18, thyroid cancer at 37.
Sole survivor of a group at Brown who called themselves
  Terminal Teens.
Emblem of fragility, just this side of poverty, mortality
  in her bones.
The harder you hit the pavement, the higher you fly

to Raymond & Zerega in the Bronx
where we play an eternal game of catch.
When her ailing, damaged world rolls down the drain by
  the gutter.
I hold her feet, lower her in.
She reaches out with humor, peers with insight,
plucks meaning from the gutter like a lost Spaldeen.

Joe Gould

Raising his glass, Joe Gould proclaimed
I suffer from delusions of grandeur!
I believe myself to be Joe Gould.

Trading stories for drinks
the 1950s eccentric set out to write an
Oral History of Our Time,

I could see the whole thing in my mind,
bushwa, gab, palaver, hogwash, flapdoodle, and malarkey,
he mused, as he poured ketchup on an empty plate
under his portrait at the Minetta Tavern.
Ketchup! The world's only free food!

But no one has ever seen that manuscript, Mr. Gould.

I'm writing for my own amusement — totally unschooled —
Because, well, I happen to be the only Joe Gould in this
  solar system
though there are probably other systems full of Joe Goulds —
a possibility I don't wish to exclude.

Dick Zigun

Here's to you, Dick Zigun,
Yale Playwright who defined Honky Tonk as the
  opposite of Hoity Toity.
then leased a building on the Coney Island Boardwalk
stood in front of Sideshows by the Seashore in an
  antique bathing suit
ballying Otis the Frog Boy till it closed at 10:30.

When Kathryn told him, *I love that place*
he claimed, *I am that place.*

He was that place for 40 years.
*Now, everything is going franchise everything is
  disappearing.*
The loss is the loss of a certain type of person
*because it's no longer seen as a noble pursuit to
  run a place that's quirky*

*I'm blessed to wave the freak flag for a whole
  liberating energy*
*for the 50,000 people who think the Mermaid Parade
  is cool*
Going topless even if your tits now sag.
*I defend the right to be tattooed on your face or have
  a pierced tongue,*
*even though you're a teenage suburban girl from
  Long Island.*
*Someone's got to carry the flag, declare this freak
  show worthy.*

Michael Roberson of the House
of Maison-Margiela

Ballroom is the struggle for freedom in the face of catastrophe,
a revolution of hope. ~ Michael Roberson

Michael — icon, pioneer and oral historian
  of House Ballroom
honors the beautiful black trans women — invisible-ized —
marginalized even within the gay & black communities —
who invented Ballroom's imaginary realms and
  creative traditions
to keep from going insane —

Trans Mother Crystal founded the House of La Beija just
  a few years after Stonewall,
inspired the Mothers and Fathers of the House of
  Dorian Corey, Ebony, Xtravaganza
proclaiming a new sexual freedom, promenading
  ornamented bodies,
voguing down ballroom runways with no shame.

Michael of the House of Maison-Margiela —
begins his oral history interviews asking the
  Mothers and Fathers
for a memory of the hallowed ballroom moments
when they achieved their soaring status —
star — statement — legend — icon — pioneer — hall of fame
to counteract — society's disdain

ends each interview asking
when the curtain closes and the lights go down,
how do you wish to be remembered?
his friend, icon Odu Adamu aka Kwame says

I upped the game.

Benjy Melendez

watches over the Bronx.

Outside the bodegas, the churches, the 99 cent shops
a Latino war chief of the Spades
tells a young initiant to aim a revolver at his temple.
twirl the barrel of the gun —
distorted initiation,
a gang leader's twisted notion of fun.

Later, the barrel turns.
A boy from the Immortals drops

The pin on his jacket, Benjy said,
it's the Puerto Rican flag, my Brother.

Benjy organized a meeting of the gangs.
Someone shouts — *hey the cops*
just want us to OFF ourselves
while they stand around and watch

This is where the violence stops, Benjy cried.

Benjy Melendez watches over the Bronx

Phyllis

Played Marian the Librarian
in our high school's Music Man.

I took her to the prom on a visit home from college.
She refused my goodnight kiss,
We went our separate ways.

Both of us tried to change the world
raising funds for vital causes.

Half a century passes, pauses
for us to gather, commiserate, work
to bring together arts and public health.

I said *you are a true success story*
She said *we both have had our say*

People have a hard time saying no to me, she said.
I sold a lot of girl scout cookies in my day

Joan's Blues

Daddy said, *girl, don't have to do nothin' in
 this world but die*
Yeah, Daddy said, *girl, don't have to do nothin'
 in this world but die*
*If you can't change the world, you damn
 sure better die tryin'*

*There's a child will change the world,
 I know that to be true*
*There's a child will change the world,
 I know that to be true*
I just hope I live to see it before my time is through.

*If they knew that child's name, they'd sound
 the great alarm*
*If they knew that child's name, they'd sound
 the great alarm*
*Shoot that child down — in her loving
 mother's arms*

April

As I run to snag the last train from Grand Central,
a disheveled, homeless woman taps my shoulder.
I spin around to see her.

I'm April, she says.
Thank you for acknowledging me.

Touched, I hand her a dollar
thinking how I've known so many
who crave acknowledgment of their existence
in the hurried indifference of this town.

With just minutes before the last train,
I recognize — her utterance was a gift.
I rush back to give her all my cash — five dollars

Tapping her shoulder, I say *April*.

She turns,
Thank you for remembering my name.

for Elaine Norman, with Zev Shanken

Elaine

The world of art
may have no heart
so you gave New York your own —
chatting with the newspaper vendor
ice cream man, the guard at the museum,

snapping pictures of iconic coffee shops,
marzipan in store windows

painting the planets revolving round the crown
    of your Easter Bonnet
as you promenade down Fifth Avenue

Ah, but in the art world — *don't even start, Elaine!*

Throw it a flippant sayonara
as you sashay down funky Broadway
transforming every part — into a work of art,

the city's old metal bridges become —
    your sparkling tiaras.

for Jim Bergman and my ping pong pals

Mr. Manhattan

The Korean waitress at the Japanese restaurant
fell in love with Jim
who always orders a Manhattan —
rye whiskey, sweet vermouth, topped with a cherry

When he is not with us, the waitress asks,
Where is Mr. Manhattan?

Here today, Jim plays the rogue.
Looking up from the Japanese menu,
  he orders a Big Mac —
the waitress tries to hold back giggles —
  she's so shy.

When we pay our share of the bill,
he holds a twenty to the light,
assuring her that, among the lot of us,
he alone will protect her from counterfeit deception.

When he leaves,
she bows as he walks by

Jim

The funniest man I ever met was a screen writer.

Bury me in my tuxedo, he said
so when the film I worked on all my life
battered by the boundless ignorance of the world
is screened at last, loved and feted, finally appreciated

dig me up!

You and John will walk me down the aisle arm in arm,
lead me to the stage

Not a soul will know I'm dead — we'll put aside
  that nasty rumor
as the Academy declares "the winner is —
  Jim Bergman — for

'Best Sense of Humor.'"

for Sally Yarmolinsky

Sally

kneeling on the rumpled bed
on her last night on earth,
Sally —

comfortable in polka dots
ruby lips and big red hats —
gloriously gaudy Sally

her face, now ghastly white

unearthed
a tube of lipstick
looked death in the mirror
applied the color smooth and bright

Disproving Death

Found Poem

One
quiet
morning,
it
will
never
be
the
same

When I'm Wobbly, Steady Me

As the vagaries of age
find new ways to trip us up
let's step over tree roots,
sidestep ice

Like a drop of dew
holds to a shaky blade of grass
I'll take your arm.

Like an autumn leaf clings to a twig,
you take mine.

Hold tight — as we sway in the breeze,
bend to winds of time.
Steady, as we go arm in arm,
into a dark — yet gentle — night.

The Pain that Walks Beside Me

The pain that walks beside me
I keep at arms length

Like a skeleton traipsing alongside me,
mocking my gait,
carrying the baggage of age,

my sidekick
whacks me hard.

I try to keep the pain beside me
so it doesn't get inside me,

define me.

Death is a Narrow Passage

like a frog hypnotized by a snake
you approach death

haunted by the narrow passage

your body's painful
squeeze into the
cold womb of
earth

cramming through
the rathole of death

toward your un-birth

Potter's Wheel

Two hands — life and death
shape eternity's clay
on the potter's wheel.

Hands caress consciousness into being,
pour in cognizance, sentience
the sense that   I   love   you

till consciousness abates
sentience evaporates.

Yet the fired clay retains the shape
of the lives poured from its lip.
Contours of a love well-lived remain
Eternal, self-contained

adapted with permission from Erika Brady's essay,
"The Beau Geste: Shaping Private Rituals of Grief,"
American Folklife Annual, 1987.

Beau Geste

dead husband's tobacco pipes
urn with father's ashes
bone ring that swelled and broke off the finger
  of a secret married lover following his suicide

Agnes sends the pipes out to sea on a little cardboard
  boat in honor of her husband. . . .
Nina arranges for the bone ring she had given her
  lover to be secretly slipped into his coffin. . . .
Catherine travels to the Sahara to scatter her father's
  ashes on the sands. . . .

Erika calls each — a private ritual of grief —
  a *Beau Geste* —
grand gesture — "brandished over irreparable loss
expressing the enormity of grief" —

action of a solitary soul whose whoosh of breath
sends a ring of ripples through the cosmos
"quietly praising — the power — of life in death."

Gossamer Bridge

The human unit of time, writes Margaret Mead,
reaches from a grandfather's memory of
  his own childhood
to a grandson's knowledge of those memories

As each generation slips away,
memories become the threads of stories,
a web of tales that spans the generations

jokes and family yarns to follow,
strung out cross the abyss
threads connecting yesterday with tomorrow

After each loss, we take first steps across
  that storied span
test our footing — wondering if our crossing
can bear — the weight of sorrow.

A Boy on a Boat in the Universe

framed on my bedroom wall —
a boy on a boat in the universe

wandering a blue green world
fading into water
conscious of the sea

from the space beneath my eyelids
the lad and I embark

through shipwrecked waters
rainbow-colored eels
towards a darkness darker than the dark

The Old, Age

until the only question left is this:
will I mourn for you
at *your* funeral
or will you — mourn for me — at *mine?*

Is it best to outlive your friends —
none left to mourn for you
Tolerate grief time after time

or spare the grief,
die first and hope they'll keep you briefly
in their hearts and minds.

which way to cut the cord
of lives so intertwined?

Instead, old friend, let's sign a pact
I'll come to your funeral — if you'll come to mine

Shadowed

I feel the ancient footsteps, like the motion of the sea
Sometimes I turn around and someone's there,
sometimes it's only me. ~ Bob Dylan, "Every Grain of Sand"

Out for dinner
on his 78th birthday
my friend — struggling through
stage four cancer — said

as I think about dying
I feel there's someone
just a few steps behind me —
a shadowy figure
who at times appears
then disappears.

Might it be the Reaper looming?
A mystic rabbi?

Not wanting to sound the alarm
I ask playfully
Is he dressed to the 9's?
maybe wearing a bowler hat?

Well, he's certainly not wishing me
happy birthday,
I can tell you that.

Life Ends

before it ends.

detach the final days —
debilitating illness
skeleton pushing through skin

My time is up
before I can will — my life to end.

this is not me, friend —
look for me around the bend

the umbilical's been severed
from the other end

Poetry

is the kiss of death, the editor said.
The public will never embrace it.

But the poem embraces me.
I'll be working on these lyrics
till I take my final breath

not unlike my father-in-law
dying in his living room who asked me
to read from *101 Favorite Poems*

Now, it's my soul
the angels circle.
Well, let them circle,
let them wait!

till I commend my soul to poetry
so I can accept the kiss of death

I am the ashes

just before the fire. . .
jogging by the sea
surfing on foam
dancing on sand

to the whale's song
the seagull's cry

wrapped in water,
soaked in wind

till the ashes of my body
scatter from the sky

with Bob Holman and Yoruba priest,
Michael Mansfield

Oyá Breathes

As you lie dying,
struggling for breath,
know that Oyá, Orisha of Winds,
the One who blows the treetops,
ruffles the mighty seas,
trembles the leaves
breathing in, breathing out—

is with you.

Rattle of death
faltering last breath
Oyá

is with you!

Exhale deeply as you can.
Your dying breath is
the Goddess breathing in
breathing in, breathing in,
exhaling to another world
that only now begins.

Farewell

I always knew it would come to this someday.

When we sold the house,
I left the rooms that shaped me,
the armchair that followed the contours of my body
as I worked on all these poems

gazed at my favorite painting on my bedroom
  wall before I slept,
two cats purring on the edge of the bed,
or stretched out on the rug by the fire

As I shuffle down the road
the house and trees grow smaller

Life distances itself from me,

I can only remember the memories —
memories of memories that slowly fade

until I can no long touch the life we had together —
conjure up a single day.

even the past grows smaller. . .
or perhaps just farther away

Learning to Live with Spirits

Upon my death,
I bequeath to each of you who loved my
  disappearing soul —
a magician's cloak — to conjure me in memory.

Proceed with a light touch —
tip your hat, wave your cloak across the table —
like a bouquet of roses my recalcitrant spirit
  reappears
leaving the audience of mourners astonished,
  hushed.

invoke our favorite punchlines
with a magician's slight of hand

Levitate a memory till my spirit lingers in the air
(the secret to the trick
is that we loved each other so so much)

Though the swords of death
skewer the swordbox
My spirit lies curled around the blades, untouched

Essays

Photo by Sarah Dargan

Beneath the Visiting Moon
Poetry to Ease the Final Passage

"We all have to face this thing sometime," my wife's father, Lucas Dargan, told me around the time he turned ninety-nine.

Six months later, he found himself facing precisely that "thing." A retired forester who planted over two million trees in his lifetime, he had split wood every morning.

Tonight, he lay in bed at the McCleod hospital in Florence, South Carolina, unable to properly swallow or get out of bed unassisted. Family members took turns staying overnight with him, and this night was my turn. At one point, I thought he was sleeping. I was working on my computer, when I heard lines from a poem coming from the other side of the room:

I am dying, Egypt, dying
Ebbs the crimson life-tide fast,
And the dark Plutonian shadows
Gather on the evening blast

"I think it's from Shakespeare," he told me, so I brought my laptop over to his bedside and looked up the lines. Born in 1917, Lucas was always amazed at the magic of the internet to access any tidbit of knowledge. The verse turned out to be from a poem by William Haines Lytle inspired by Shakespeare's *Antony and Cleopatra*. The first line, "I am dying, Egypt, dying," is from the play itself. We then looked up the drama online and found Marc Antony's soliloquy that begins with that line. Then I read to him from Shakespeare's play.

When I finished, he said, "Steve, when I close my eyes I think of the billions of people who have done this before me."

"Well, you know you'll be remembered," I said.

"That's true," he said, "not as good as heaven—but a lot better than hell."

The next day the doctor told Lucas and the family that there was nothing more to be done medically and recommended hospice care. That day, we brought Lucas home to the family farm and set up his bed in the living room, where for the next three weeks he was surrounded by family members and a stream of visitors, including guests for the weekly poetry and music nights he had hosted at the house for many years. Other visitors included members of his old Boy Scout troop, who talked about what they had learned from him, and a local farmer, David White, who had started a tradition of bringing lunch to share with Lucas every Monday, and who this time brought in a newborn duckling.

Among his many visitors was the hospice chaplain. Lucas couldn't help but share his view of religion with him: "I do not claim to understand the nature of the Supreme Being, and I do not acknowledge that anyone else does either."

Photo by Rosa Dargan Powers.

Lucas was a devoted agnostic who believed that it was just as much a leap of faith to be an atheist as a believer. The chaplain, who returned for a second visit, said he enjoyed discussing spirituality with Lucas and concluded, "He just doesn't want to put God in a box."

It was clear to all of us that in his final days Lucas sought solace in poetry, not religion. He told my wife, Amanda, "I think all poets share a deep concern for the human condition." And the poets whose works he wanted to hear or to recite were those who wrote about death and dying and those whose poems he had memorized when he was young.

Many of the poems he knew by heart, including some we had never heard him recite before. Once, when I asked if he wanted me to read a poem, he said, "Steve, look up Carruth."

"Carruth?" I said.

"Yes, *C-a-r-r-u-t-h*, William Herbert Carruth."

The poem he had in mind, "Each in His Own Tongue," seemed to capture Lucas's poetic perspective on religion. I picked up his tattered copy of *One Hundred and One Famous Poems*, published in 1924. I read a line from the poem, "A haze on the far horizon." Lying in his bed, he recited the second from memory, "The infinite, tender sky." I read the third line, and then he responded with the fourth from memory. We went all through the poem in tandem.

The ripe, rich tint of the cornfields,
And the wild geese sailing high —
And all over the upland and lowland
The charm of the goldenrod —
Some of us call it Autumn,
And others call it God.

A day or two later, he asked Amanda to read the poem "Thanatopsis" by William Cullen Bryant, another classic 19th century poem about death.

. . . When thoughts
Of the last bitter hour come like a blight
Over thy spirit, and sad images
Of the stern agony, and shroud, and pall,
And breathless darkness, and the narrow house,
Make thee to shudder, and grow sick at heart . . .

As she read, Amanda watched her father close his eyes. She thought he had drifted off to sleep, and she put the book down, too sad to continue. When he opened his eyes a few minutes later, her sister Rosa asked, "Would you like to hear another poem?"

"Not yet," he said. "Amanda hasn't finished the one she was reading."

Rosa finished reading Bryant's poem.

By an unfaltering trust, approach thy grave
Like one who wraps the drapery of his couch
About him, and lies down to pleasant dreams.

Lucas draped himself in the weave of his favorite poems as he confronted death, as if he could pull them up like a blanket. They kept him warm and clearly helped him approach his death with peace of mind. His amazing mind — "fastened to a dying animal," as Yeats put it — remained sharp until the end. He didn't stop reciting and listening to poems until the day before he died. "We should all aspire to his life — and his death," his nephew Rod McIver said.

As befitted this man, his daughters planned the funeral service to include his grandchildren reading some of his favorite poems, including Shelley's "The Cloud," Masefield's "Sea Fever," and Tennyson's "Crossing the Bar." The service closed with his poetry-night stalwarts — Stanley Thompson, David Brown, and Worth Lewellyn — playing his favorite song, "Loch Lomond," on fiddle and guitar. ("You take the high road and I'll take the low and I'll get to Scotland before you . . . ")

I was left mulling over the lines we had read together from Shakespeare's Antony and Cleopatra.

This case of that huge spirit now is cold . . .
And there is nothing left remarkable
Beneath the visiting moon.

How Do You Wear the Universe?

Imagine this. We are traveling on a train at night and pass by a village with a row of brightly lit houses behind a row of evenly spaced trees. As our train whizzes past, it appears as if the lights of the houses are flickering on and off, as the trees block and then reveal them. In our lifespans we move through time like that train passing by the tree-lined streets. It appears that people are born, die, and disappear forever. They flare up, flicker, and are extinguished. But if we imagine our lives as the lights in these houses, there is a sense in which they remain forever lit.

In March, 1955, Einstein heard that his close friend and frequent sounding board, Michele Besso, passed away in his eighties. Einstein wrote a letter to Besso's sister which he ended this way: "Now he has departed from this strange world a little ahead of me. That means nothing. People like us, who believe in physics, know that the distinction between past, present, and future is only a stubbornly persistent illusion."

My sense is that we are all granted a permanent place on the continuum of time.

When Viktor Frankl writes about the Holocaust in *Man's Search for Meaning*, he echoes a parallel sentiment:

> *Those things which seem to take meaning away from human life include not only suffering but dying as well. I never tire of saying that the only really transitory aspects of life are the potentialities; but as soon as they are actualized, they are rendered realities at that very moment; they are saved and delivered into the past, wherein they are rescued and preserved from transitoriness. For, in the past, nothing is irretrievably lost but everything irrevocably stored.* [1]

In order not to take ourselves too seriously, I joked with my lifelong friend, the late Sol Reuben, a therapist, that everyone is entitled to their own cracker-barrel philosophy as long as they don't seek to impose it on others. We call this principle "crackerbarrelism." This leads us to debate, for instance, his Buddhist perspective, which views the universe as a symphony without a conductor, versus my own point of view, in which each individual conducts his own symphony.

Sol and I were fond of quoting Sholem Aleichem's wonderful line, "Let my name be recalled with laughter or not at all." We argued, in true crackerbarrel style, about a cartoon that shows a Buddha by a river seeing his reflection in the water as a clown — but leaving it unclear whether it's about a Buddha who sees himself as a clown, or a clown who sees himself as Buddha — or both. Does the clown dive into the pool in search of his spirtual self? Or does the Buddha squeeze into a clown car and drive away? It's hard to tell which image is above or below the waterline. Turn the cartoon upside down for answers.

From the cracker-barrel of idiocyncratic philosophies, this essay speaks to what I believe to be eternal qualities of our being — and our art.

A Permanent Existence in the Subtle Folds of Time

Contemporary science suggests that time is a fourth dimension. We can easily picture the three dimensions of length, width, and depth. If we are meeting someone in an office building, for instance, we need to give these three dimensions: two horizontal and one vertical dimension (the street, the cross-street, and the floor of the building), but we also need to give the time of the meeting. If we miss the meeting, we can go back to the same place, but never at the exact time and date. We find it more difficult to envision time as a dimension that we're moving through much as we move through space, partly because, from our vantage point as human beings, we move through chronological time at a fixed pace in only one direction. The timeline flows only forward. If we can bend our minds to picture that fourth dimension the same way we picture the other three, and to imagine we move through time the same way we move through space, it's easier to envision an eternal quality to our lives.

A new theory by University of Alaska Fairbanks scientist Gunther Kletetschka argues that time itself exists in three dimensions rather than just the single one we experience as continual forward progression in only one direction. In a recent exposition of the theory in *Sci News*, Victor Davis Hanson writes "Imagine you are walking down a straight path, moving forward and therefore experiencing time as we know it. Now imagine another path that crosses the first one, going sideways. If you could step onto that sideways path and remain in the same moment of regular time, you might find that things could be slightly different — perhaps a different version of the same day. The new approach," Kletschka suggests, "might even help resolve the grandest of all unresolved physics challenges: unifying quantum mechanics — the behavior of particles at the smallest scales — and gravity into a single quantum theory of gravity. A quantum theory of gravity could lead to, or become, a grand theory of the Universe — the so-called theory of everything."[2] The very thing Einstein was searching for. Scientists, like poets, are still seeking....

Cosmic Memory

Memory takes us a miniscule way across spacetime because it enables us to access our past, takes us back to things remembered in our own lives. Kurt Vonnegut goes further in his novel *Slaughterhouse-Five*, in which the protagonist, Billy Pilgrim, becomes "unstuck in time."[3] But as we age our memories, too, become unstuck in time.

We give our personal lives meaning through memory. Even our bad memories teach us lessons in memorable ways. I believe the more we validate our life-affirming memories, the more meaningful our lives seem to us. Life's task, then, becomes the validation of memory. Long before we're relegated to the dementia unit of the hospital, we are tasked with memory care.

As Faulkner put it, "The past is never dead. It's not even past."

I tried to capture my own sense of this conundrum in a few lines I called "Ghosts of Future Past":

> *Once*
> *At the juncture*
> *Of anticipation and memory*
> *A gesture, a smile, a kiss . . .*
> *Though it seems long gone*
> *What happened, is.*

Our perceptions of time are built into our language, with its present, past, and future tenses. You'll know I'm dead, the moment you hear someone say, "Steve was…" But I believe even when I'm dead, dead dead, there is a sense in which Steve still "is." This is the way I contemplate "my future deadness."[4]

A life, then, is a little like a photograph slipped into the recesses of time, retained in the DNA of the time continuum.

As the poet Mary Oliver writes, "I look upon time as no more than an idea, and consider eternity as another possibility."[5]

Not surprisingly, many of my friends are skeptical of this view, including the poet Tsaurah Litzky, who wrote in her poem "Sour Milk," "I struggle against my anger at life, the ultimate bad joke, with the worst punch line—eternal darkness."

Not necessarily. I jotted down these lines, which also appear earlier in the book, to sum up our disagreement:

She said, *Your life means nothing once you're dead*

He said, *No, it's written down*
inscribed onto the cosmos
scrawled in the margins of time

She said, *But inaccessible to humankind*

Yet permanent, still there
like a book. I said

She replied,
A book nobody reads

Of course, if everybody read everybody else's "life books," they wouldn't have time for much else. Tsaurah, on receiving this poem, responded with some additional lines:

written down
inscribed in the cosmos, Ha!
where in the cosmos can
I find inscribed the lives
of my dear mother and father?
what language will their lives
be written in?

You have a point, Tsaurah. Yet, perhaps our lives remain present just as they happened, in the same language as life. Sorry to say, there is no way to access them, trapped as we are in the human condition.

Intimations of Immortality: Eternal Dimensions in Art

For me, there are, as Wordsworth put it so well, "intimations of immortality" not only in our creative lives and memories but in the art we create. In stories and jokes and poems and visual art I find the clearest manifestations of the eternal. Medicine show doc Fred Bloodgood, a purveyor of magnificent hyperboles, put it this way:

> I'll say that when the last grand cataclysm of Earth's disintegration resounds with thunderous cacophony, as bursting stars and blazing fragments go hissing into uncharted stratosphere, the medicine show will still live in our hearts forever."[6]

I feel that way about poetry and art. Even if the planet comes to a crashing, cataclysmic end, and all our creative works are destroyed by ice or fire, these structures of meaning and feeling embodied in poems and art will still continue to exist somewhere between the ozone and the ether.

Often art seems to develop an agency of its own, apart from its creator. Once the idea for a poem zaps across the synapses of my brain, the work seems to develop an independent will. As my friend the poet Bob Holman puts it, "Let the poem be what it wants to be. That's poetry's essence." This speaks to the way any work of art begins, with a thought, observation, or insight about the world, or one's experience in it, but harbors its own structure of meaning and feeling. That structure is what enables it to resonate beyond its creator; in some sense it continues to exist this way, as its own entity, into eternity.

As the Hawaiian storyteller Nyla Fujii-Babb puts it: "You don't own [stories] . . . the stories don't belong to us. They're not ours. They are, of themselves, their own entity."[7]

Poems and stories, written or told, seem to me to be particles of meaning, like the atom or the molecule. Just as human cells do, they contain something like the DNA of their creators.

> *The universe is made of stories, not atoms,*
> writes the poet Muriel Rukeyser,
>
> to which the Buddhist writer David Loy responds,
> *Not atoms?*
>
> *Of course it is made of atoms.*
> *That's one of our most important stories.*[8]

Great poems and stories are a bit like an atom, indestructible — put together so tightly, they are able to destroy the universe, blown apart if a word or brush stroke were taken out of place. My own poems come together when two disparate thoughts or ideas come crashing together. Working through what joins those divergent thoughts together creates the poem — the process, a kind of atomic fusion.

John Berger writes:

> *If poetry sometimes speaks of its own immortality, the claim is more far-reaching than that of the genius of a particular poet in a particular cultural history. Immortality here should be distinguished from posthumous fame. Poetry can speak of immortality because it abandons itself to*

language, in the belief that language embraces all experience, past, present, and future....

Poetry can repair no loss but it defies the space which separates. And it does this by its continual labor of reassembling what has been scattered. . . . [9]

When considered in this way, poems appear to push back the boundaries of mortality.

As the Jewish theologian Abraham Joshua Heschel writes, they weave "the threads of temporality into the fabric of eternity."[10]

Infinities Nestled in Time

I have always been struck by the eternalism in everyday things. In the book (and motion picture adaptation) *The Fault in Our Stars*, author John Green has his character Hazel, a sixteen-year-old dying of cancer, offer some intriguing thoughts on a short life while speculating on the nature of infinity. As she plans a eulogy for her boyfriend, also dying of cancer, she states "There are infinite numbers between 0 and 1. There's .1 and .12 and .112 and an infinite collection of others. Of course, there is a bigger infinite set of numbers between 0 and 2, or between 0 and a million. Some infinities are bigger than other infinities. . . . I cannot tell you how grateful I am for our little infinity. You gave me forever within the numbered days, and I'm grateful."[11]

I'm reminded of Liza Lister, who, though she died at the age of 6, seemed to understand this.

Liza Lister

Carefree little squirt
Diagnosed with leukemia at the age of four
Who, in an act of will, lived to be six,
brave little girl, who asked to die on her mother's lap
listening to her favorite lullabye.

She loved cows, milk by the quart.
Concluded, I've had a good life,
Only short

A math blogger, Yen Duong, in her "Baking and Math" blog, disputes the mathematics behind Hazel's sweet sentiment about infinity, illustrating the proof that all infinities are, in fact, the same size. She ends up offering her own, mathematically sounder way of looking at longer and shorter lives in relation to infinity: "Whether those different sorts of infinities apply to something like moments of time is unknown. What we do know is that if life has infinite moments, or infinite love, or infinite being, then a life twice as long still has exactly the same amount. Some infinities only look bigger than other infinities."[12]

Let Us Conjure Meaning

Are the ideas of poets and artists who address eternity parallel to the beautiful and simply expressed proofs and formulas of scientists? Are these poetic ideas about the nature of time actually etched onto the physical universe? Is it inconsistent to jump from Proust's conception of the "eternal now," or the Brazilian poet Vinicius de Moraes's wonderful line "infinite while it lasts," to Einstein's idea that "the distinction between past, present and future is only an illusion?"

It's as if I'm looking down a set of railroad tracks. On one track are the insights of scientists about the illusive nature of time; on the other are the thoughts and dreams of poets with their intimations of immortality. As I gaze into the distance, the two tracks seem to run together as if they were joined in a kind of optical illusion created by perspective. They run together as they fade towards the horizon, serving to suggest that our lives are both poetic and, in some cosmic sense, eternal.

Yet I have to admit that beyond the vanishing point of the horizon, the two tracks may continue to run on apart. Perhaps the "human unit of time" and the passing of stories across the generations are indeed the best we have to look forward to on the "flowering side of the dirt."

I've relied on friends to share life's meanings — to satisfy the "lust for meaning" within me. A dear friend once told me that the only meaning of life is keeping busy. I disagree, vehemently. Folklorist Dan Sheehy said, the only meaning of life is the meaning you give it. An English professor of mine at Bucknell, Dr. Withim, told my class, Life Means Enormously.

An ancient Jewish story sums it up best. Here it is as a poem,

> Why must a Jew always answer a question
>   with a question?
> Because a good question is half the answer,
> and because a shtetl student,
> studying by candlelight,
> screamed suddenly,
>
> What is the meaning of life?
>
> He ran to wake the rabbi in the middle of the night.

The rabbi smacked him.

You have such a beautiful question.
Why would you exchange it for an answer?

Perhaps the search for meaning turns out to be the meaning.
As my friend Bob Holman wrote,

> *And so the philosophical, philological,*
> *semiotical, deconstructivist, poets*
> *argued late into the night.*
>
> *What's the meaning of meaning?*
> *What's the purpose of purpose?*
>
> *Oh, I get it, one said. The answer's*
> *not related to the question,*
> *and nothing's on purpose,*
>
> *the purpose of which is to assure you*
> *that's there's no meaning to meaning in the first place.*
>
> *But in the second place . . .*

The harshest critic of my sometimes overly buoyant credos is my dear friend, Marc Kaminsky. Addressing me in the third person (as it is appropriate for the critic to do), Marc once wrote in the margins of an early draft of this chapter, "Zeitlin tightly equates spirit with the eternal, and the eternal as indestructible—a thoroughly Western conception. He conflates the experience of the eternal with its literalization as described in scientific concepts. Spirit can also be seen as Tao, as a force moving through the universe continually. For me Zeitlin's fallacy is to equate eternity with permanence (very Western). In the east, in Taoism and Buddhism, eternity is associated with impermanence, with Yin

Yang alternations of creation and destruction moving through the endlessness of time."

Ultimately, Marc rephrased my ideas in a way that made sense to him: "The artist's secular sphere of spirituality occurs at the intersection of time and timelessness. Our goal is not a denial of death, but to hold eternity and death in a single thought."

The artist's secular sphere of spirituality has always been my home address.

Amen, Marc

Endnotes

1 Viktor E. Frankl, *Man's Search for Meaning* (Boston: Beacon Press, 1959, 2006), 120.

2 See https://www.sci.news/physics/three-dimensional-time-14011.html #google_vignette.

3 See Kurt Vonnegut, *Slaughterhouse-Five* (New York: Dell Publishing, 1991.

4 Ruth Rosengarten, *Second Chances: My Life in Things*, 2022.

5 Mary Oliver, "When Death Comes," in *New and Selected Poems* (Boston: Beacon Press, 1992), 10.

6 *Free Show Tonight,* a documentary by Paul Wagner and Steve Zeitlin (1982), streamed on Folkstreams.net.

7 Transcribed by Milbre Burch from archival recordings for The Storytelling Project of the Cotsen Children's Library.

8 David Loy, *The World Is Made of Stories* (Somerville, Mass.: Wisdom Press, 2010), 3.

9 John Berger, *And Our Faces, My Heart, Brief as Photos* (New York: Vintage Books, 1984), 22, 96–97.

10 Abraham Joshua Heschel, *Moral Grandeur and Spiritual Audacity: Essays* (New York: Farrar, Straus and Giroux, 1997), 378.

11 John Green, *The Fault in Our Stars* (New York: Penguin Books, 2014), 260.

12 Evelyn Lamb, "Some Infinities Are Bigger Than Other Infinities, and Some Are Just the Same Size," http://blogs. scientificamerican.com, July 10, 2014.

About the Author

Steve Zeitlin is a folklorist, writer, poet, songwriter, ping pong player, and cultural activist. Steve is the Founding Director of City Lore, New York's center for urban folk culture, celebrating its 40th anniversary this year. City Lore works with grassroots cultures to ensure their living legacy in stories and histories, places and traditions. In 2002, Steve co-founded the Brevitas poetry collective, dedicated to the short poem. In 2007, he received the Benjamin Botkin Award from the American Folklore Society for lifetime achievement in public folklore. Steve Zeitlin has served as a regular commentator for a number of nationally syndicated public radio shows, and his commentaries have appeared on the Op Ed pages of *The New York Times* and *Newsday*.

Prior to arriving in New York, Steve Zeitlin served for eight years as a folklorist at the Smithsonian Institution and has taught at George Washington, American University, NYU, and Cooper Union. He is coauthor of a number of award-winning books on America's folk culture, as well as coproducer or codirector of a number of acclaimed film documentaries including *Free Show Tonight* on the traveling medicine shows of the l920s and 30s; *From Mambo to Hip Hop; Deaf Jam,* about American Sign Language poets; *The Grand Generation: Memory, Mastery, Legacy; Let's Get the Rhythm: the Life and Times of Miss Mary Mack;* and *In the Moment: Poetry Duels from Around the World*, with his wife, folklorist Amanda Dargan.